ALLEN PHOTOGRAPHIC GUIDES

THE CAVALIER KING CHARLES SPANIEL

CONTENTS

BREED DESCRIPTION

CHARACTER

Affectionate, friendly, sporting, fearless and non-aggressive; all these words have been used to describe the Cavalier King Charles Spaniel, Britain's most popular small dog. There are many reasons for this popularity and the most important is the Cavalier temperament.

A Cavalier is never happier than when he has human companionship and this can be with children (preferably three years old or older), the parents and the grandparents. The Cavalier really enjoys being with you, in fact he needs to be with you. In the house, sitting on your lap, or sleeping on the floor at your feet while you're watching television, playing with children indoors or outside in the garden, riding with you in the car when you go shopping, or on a longer trip, Cavaliers are truly 'companion' dogs, and a new puppy will quickly bond with a family when he joins it. It has been said that Cavaliers have a big dog's temperament in a small frame. They are full of fun and easily adapt to a town or country environment. They are equally pleased to doze in the room where you are, or join you for a walk.

However, they do not like to be left alone for long periods. They will soon become bored and start to bark and chew furniture or get up to some other mischief. If your life style prevents you from providing sufficient companionship for your Cavalier, you should consider taking on another Cavalier (but do not mix the sexes!) so that the two Cavaliers can enjoy playing and providing companionship for each other. It will mean very little extra work for you.

The Cavalier loves human company…

Tricolour dog with his frisbee

PHYSICAL CHARACTERISTICS

The Cavalier is a small dog that will grow to about 13in (30 cm) in height and will weigh between 14 to 20 lb (6 to 9 kg). He will have a silky coat and long well 'feathered' ears, all of which should be combed or brushed a few minutes every day. The tail is also well feathered, and usually wagging, another typical Cavalier trait! The head and 'soft' expression, aided by large dark eyes, give Cavaliers the typical 'melting' look that makes them so appealing.

Eighteen-month-old Blenheim at a show

Parts of the dog

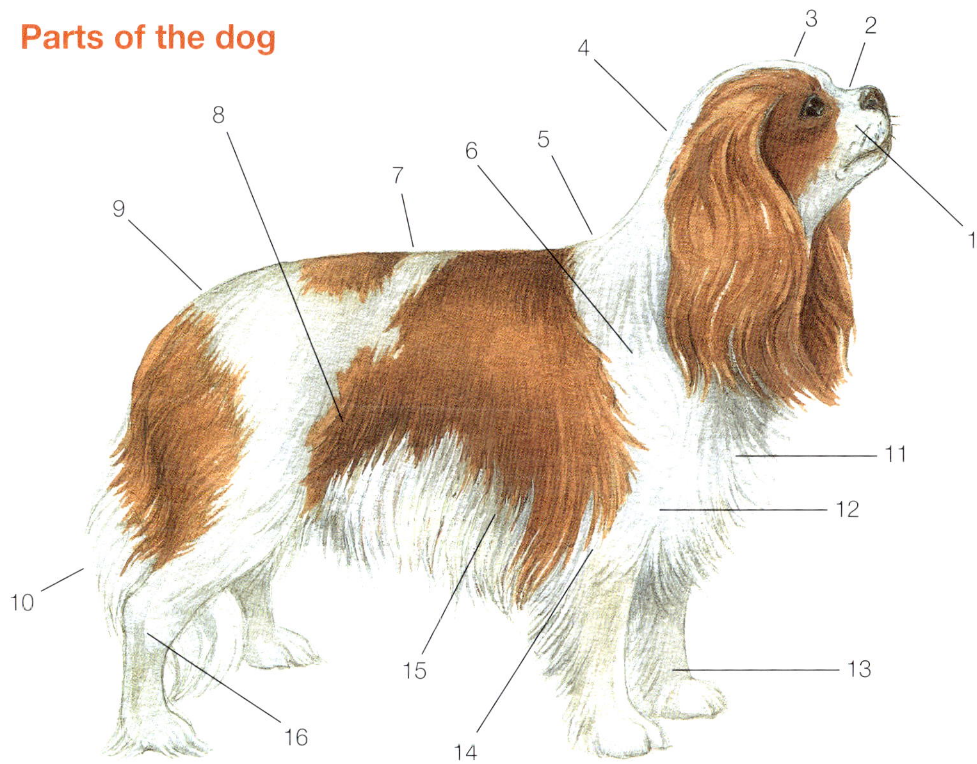

Key

1 Muzzle
2 Stop
3 Skull
4 Neck
5 Withers
6 Shoulder
7 Back
8 Loin
9 Croup
10 Tail
11 Chest
12 Upper arm
13 Pastern
14 Elbow
15 Ribcage
16 Hock

Cavaliers evolved in the 1920s and '30s from the flat-faced King Charles Spaniels that have a large 'domed' skull with ears set low on the head and a very short, turned-up nose. Cavaliers have a skull that is almost flat between the ears which are set high on the head. The nose is about 1½ in (3.8 cm) long.

The difference between the Cavalier King Charles (*left*) and the King Charles (*above*) can be seen here very clearly

COLOURS

There are four coat colours. The most common are the *Blenheims* that have a rich chestnut colour broken up on a pearly white background. The face marking should be evenly divided. Some Blenheims have a spot on the top of the head called a lozenge and some people feel this is an important marking. This is not essential, however; choose the markings that please your eye.

Blenheim

Tricolour

Ruby

Black and tan

Tricolours have black patches, well spaced, on the pearly white background. They have tan eyebrows and tan on the cheeks, the inner sides of the legs and under the tail. As the puppy grows older, there is a tendency for the black hair to override what had been white.

Rubies have a rich, red coat overall.

Black and tans are similarly marked to the tricolours except that there is no white hair in the coat at all. (There may be a few white hairs on young puppies, but they will disappear as the coat thickens.)

The rubies and black and tans are referred to as 'whole-colours', the Blenheims and tricolours as 'particolours'. A little white on whole-colours is quite acceptable if they are not going to be exhibited in the show ring. In fact, some people consider it gives the Cavalier greater personality!

CHOICE OF PUPPY

MALE OR FEMALE?

Litter of five-week-old puppies of all colours

This is an important choice. Unless you want to breed, or already own a female, you will be better off with a male. Male Cavaliers are just as affectionate as the females and want, and like, just as much attention and companionship. They are not aggressive, and will want to please their human families as much as female Cavaliers.

Female Cavaliers will be in season for three weeks at a time, twice a year. This will curtail usual outdoor activities, such as walks and will mean extra attention indoors to chairs and carpets. Having the female spayed is not a perfect solution – it can cause weight gain and a thicker, less controllable, coat. (Likewise, the neutered male also will gain weight and develop a thicker coat.)

If you intend to have two Cavaliers remember that they should be of the same sex. Resist any temptation to use your dog at stud to a neighbour's bitch. It will upset him and give him ideas and may cause him to begin to wander. If you wish to breed from your female, go to an experienced breeder who will provide stud service, guide you through the pregnancy and help you to place your puppies in good homes.

For this eight-week-old Blenheim puppy life is fun

(*above*) Seven-week-old tricolour puppy

FINDING A BREEDER

Do not buy a Cavalier puppy that you may have seen, looking so adorable, in a pet shop. Be very careful about answering a 'pups for sale' advertisement in your local newspaper. You will be much better advised to buy your puppy from an experienced Cavalier breeder who owns and lives with the parents of the puppies that are offered for sale. You can get in touch with such breeders through one of the Cavalier Clubs in the UK that will have a register of members with puppies for sale (see page 23). The Kennel Club maintains a Puppy Sales Register and will post an information pack to prospective puppy buyers. *The Dog Directory*, a magazine which lists dog breeders, is available through newsagents. It is not hard to locate Cavalier breeders, but puppies are not always immediately available.

When you have made a list of breeders to contact, there are several questions you should ask.

- Are the mother (dam) and father (sire) registered with the Kennel Club and will the puppies be registered? Registration is the only way to be certain that the puppies are pure-bred Cavaliers.
- Have the sire and dam had their hearts tested? The breeder should be able to confirm that neither parent had a heart murmur at the time they were mated.
- Were the sire and dam tested clear of eye cataracts?
- If the dam is not at home with her puppies, where is she? Check that the litter being offered is home bred, and not 'bought in'.
- Find out what price the breeder will be wanting for the puppy.

If the answers to these questions are satisfactory, you should ask if you may visit the breeders at their premises to see the litter (or puppy) and the dam. This will give you an opportunity to assess the puppy and, by looking at the dam, you will get an idea

Blenheim, mother and daughter

what the puppy will look like when adult. During this visit you can expect the breeder to ask you some simple questions as to the nature of the home that you would be offering to the puppy.

Fourteen-week-old Blenheim puppies

- Is this your first dog? Have you any previous puppy experience?
- Do you have children in your family? How old are they?
- Do you go out to work? Would the puppy be left alone for more than three hours at a time?
- Have you a garden? Is it fenced in so the puppy could not 'escape'?

When, at last, you have found 'your' puppy, and dealt successfully with the breeder, you may still have to wait as Cavaliers should not be taken from their 'nest' until they are at least eight weeks old.

Eight-week-old tricolour puppy

Mother and daughter

Seven-week-old Blenheim puppy

PUPPY CARE

HOME PREPARATION

Good examples of dog beds

You will need to make some preparations before you bring the puppy in to your home. Decide which rooms he will be allowed in, and make sure that television cables and live electrical wires have been put out of reach. For one or two weeks a cardboard box with a cut out entrance will serve as a temporary bed but the best permanent beds are the oval, plastic type which are readily available at pet centres. You will also be able to buy a fleece pad to lie in the bottom.

A metal fold-down cage is very useful. It can be used at night when you do not want the puppy to wander round the room. It is also useful during the day, for short periods, when you have to be away and it is ideal for travelling in a car. The cage will stop the puppy from jumping out if a door is not closed properly or, perish the thought, if you are involved in an accident. The puppy will feel it is a secure place of his own.

You will need a collar and lead when your puppy comes home with you. Choose a woven nylon type, about ½ in (1.2 cm) wide. As your puppy grows you should change to a soft, rolled leather collar. Do not choose a 'harness' type as it will strain the muscles in the puppy's shoulders. You will also need to get an identity disc to attach to the collar, as required by law.

Outdoors you must make sure that you have a secure area where the puppy can play. Cavaliers can wriggle through quite small areas of broken fencing. Chicken-wire netting is not to be recommended as your puppy can chew at it and could damage his teeth or mouth. A wooden fence is much better and it will reduce the risk of your puppy barking at your neighbours, who would be visible through a wire fence. Sadly, Cavaliers are

Types of cage which are ideal for travelling

An armful of six-week-old puppies

too impulsive to have much road sense, and may 'escape' through the front door when a visitor arrives. Until your puppy is older, and has had some training, make sure there is no access on to the road.

When your puppy first arrives home, do not be alarmed if he wants to sleep a lot. This rest is quite natural and will help growth. Your puppy may not eat very much the first day: he is learning about the new environment and may also be missing litter mates. It usually takes a day or two for the puppy to 'settle in'. Have some toys he can play with, such as a ball or soft toy, but take care there are no eyes or buttons that could be pulled off and swallowed. If you have small children in your household, make sure they do not overtire the puppy when they play together. Try to encourage the children to sit on the floor to play and make sure they know the correct way to hold a puppy so that he cannot wriggle and fall out of their arms (see page 12).

Two puppies will enjoy and benefit from each other's company

On the first night, when the puppy is really tired, take him outside to relieve himself and then put him into his bed or cage with a toy and a biscuit. He may cry but eventually this will stop, unless you keep returning to him in which case he will think this is fun! You should start the way you want to go on. If you once take a puppy to your bed he will expect it every night!

If you are not already registered as a client with a veterinary practice, you should do this without waiting for the first emergency. Speak to the vet when your puppy has settled in and inquire when he would recommend your puppy to be inoculated. This is usually ten to twelve weeks after the puppy's birth. At the same time, the vet will give your puppy a general check. Your puppy must not be allowed into any public places until after his inoculations. Your puppy should have been wormed by his breeder but your vet may wish to worm him again after the inoculations. He should be wormed every six months after this, throughout his adult life.

Tricolour and Blenheim puppies aged five weeks

TRAINING

HOUSE TRAINING

Try not to scold your puppy in the first few days with you, a strong 'NO' should be sufficient if required. Cavalier puppies are sensitive and need to learn from you the behaviour you want from them. They are inquisitive and always ready to try something new. On the other hand they must learn, and accept, that you are master. Do not use the bed or the cage as the place in which to punish him for bad behaviour. It should be the place in which he can feel relaxed and happy.

Once your puppy has settled in, you should start house training. Cavaliers are quick to learn and this should only take a few days, with the occasional accident.

Puppy with his new friend

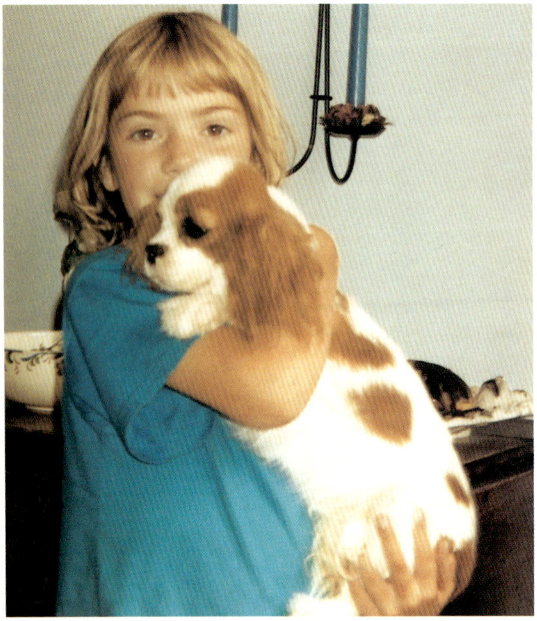

Hold the puppy under his chest and rear, holding him close to your body

Make sure that you hold his legs together and support his rear end

Whenever your puppy wakes up, or finishes a meal, you should carry him outside to the place you want him to relieve himself. Stay with him until he performs, then praise him, telling him how good he has been. Do not expect your puppy to wake up and walk from his sleeping place to go outside before he performs. Pick him up and go outside closing the door behind you. If you just put him outside, close the door, and leave him, he will be there when you open the door, walk right in, and do it! The effort you put in for the first week or two will be well rewarded.

LEAD TRAINING

The Cavalier has a strong desire to please his owner and this makes your puppy quite easy to train. Training should be done in short spells of only a few minutes, repeating the same exercise several times, and treated almost like a game. Always praise the puppy warmly, touch and make a fuss of him when the exercise is performed correctly.

Wearing a collar and walking on a lead are necessary lessons and should be learnt by the time your puppy is five months old. Start to get the puppy used to wearing a light collar by putting it around his neck every day. Leave it on for an increasing length of time, until he stops scratching and it no longer feels strange. The next step is to attach the lead to the collar. At first, let him take you along. Drop the lead if your puppy starts to 'fight'. Never drag your puppy, always encourage movement while you keep the lead loose. Gradually, and with patience on your part, the puppy will learn to follow you.

Once he is accustomed to walking on the lead, curb any tendency the puppy has to pull away from you. You can do this by walking in the opposite direction yourself. You do not want an adult Cavalier that tries to pull you along. Keep up a constant flow of encouragement and praise every success.

Introducing a puppy to a lead

SITTING

Once walking on the lead has been taught, you are ready to start training your Cavalier to sit, sit and stay, and down stay. Begin by putting the dog in the sitting position. Using a titbit, hold it above the dog's head. If he begins to stand as he looks up, move your hand back over the dog who will automatically go back into the sit position. Give the command 'SIT', in a firm voice. Praise each time. After several successful repetitions, reward the dog with the titbit. In time, your dog will learn to sit promptly on command, without you having to use the titbit.

Sit

SITTING AND STAYING

To teach your puppy to 'sit stay', command the dog to sit. Holding the lead, move a pace away and give the command 'STAY'. If the dog is unsteady, return and repeat the command. If he is steady, back away two more paces to give the 'stay' command. Remain at a distance for a short period of time, perhaps counting up to five, then walk back to your Cavalier and praise him.

Sit and stay

DOWN

To teach your dog to 'down stay', place the dog in the sit position. Using the titbit, let the dog have a sniff of what is on offer, while you slowly lower your hand and go to the down position. As you do this give the command 'DOWN' in a positive voice, and praise the dog when the exercise is complete. When settled in the down position, give the command 'STAY' and reinforce this by making a hand signal in front of the dog's face.

These training exercises should always end in a positive way with your Cavalier receiving lavish praise and a reward.

Down and stay

FEEDING

There are many varieties of proprietary dog foods on the market, all of which have been carefully prepared to provide the necessary vitamins, calcium and minerals your puppy will need. Some are made as crunchy pellets, others are tinned, cooked meats. These are readily available in supermarkets and pet shops. The breeder should have provided you with a puppy diet menu which you should follow in the first two or three weeks.

A general guide is that you should feed your puppy four times a day for the first eight to twelve weeks, three times a day at thirteen to twenty weeks, twice a day until nine months and one meal a day thereafter. You will find that some dog-food manufacturers have special preparations for puppies, juniors, adults and a maintenance menu for the elderly. These variations provide the various mineral requirements for the different ages.

We like to give two puppy biscuits to our puppies at bedtime and our 'oldies' still get this 'treat'. Remember to have fresh water available at all times.

Eight-week-old ruby puppy

GROOMING

BASIC EQUIPMENT

1 Coat brushes

2 Slicker brush – used for ears, tail and matted hair

3 Combs – may be fine or broad – for untangling hair

4 Light, nylon weave collar

5 Rolled leather collar

6 Lead with collar

7 Lead with detachable clip to collar

8 Scissors for underfoot hair between the pads

9 Nail clippers

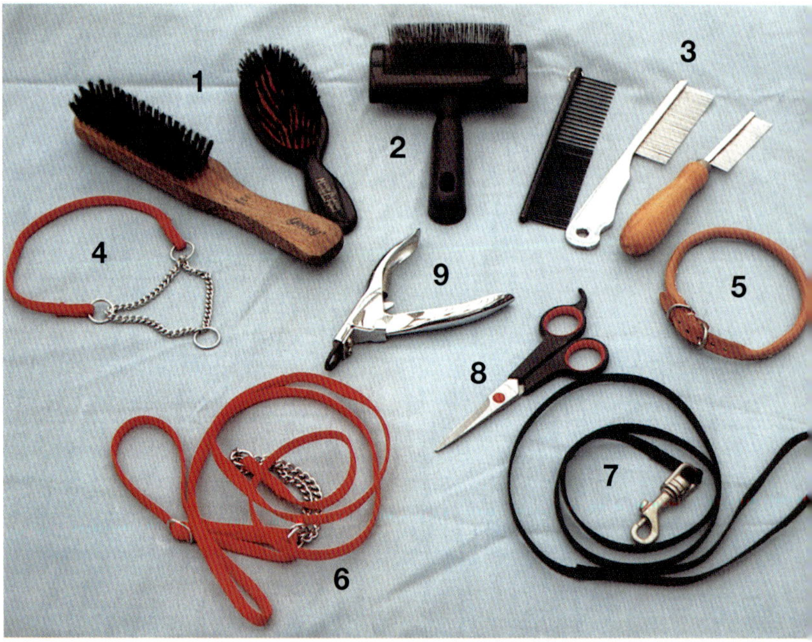

Try to establish a routine for grooming your puppy daily and get him used to it while young. It need only take about five minutes but will be enjoyed by the puppy and will help to keep him in condition. Mostly it should include combing and brushing the coat, wiping away eye-stains and keeping the ears clean. Cavaliers enjoy an occasional bath and this can be done about once a month and more frequently if the puppy has found something smelly to roll in! There are suitable shampoos available for all conditions. If the puppy is dusty or dirty after a walk, let him dry off and then give him a good brush to get rid of any mud.

Cavaliers are 'natural' dogs and their coats should not be trimmed or clipped. However, it is advisable to trim the hair that grows within the pads of the feet as, if this gets too dense, walking is uncomfortable. Neutered or spayed dogs tend to have a heavy, profuse coat, with a fluffy texture and these tend to mat more easily and take longer to comb.

Ears – You should check your puppy's ears each week to make sure they are clean and free from infection and ear mites. To do this, take a cotton wool bud and gently wipe the inside of the ear (do not poke down further than you can see). If there is a dark brown stain on the bud you will require ear-drops, which are available from your vet.

Cleaning the ears

Eyes – Wipe the corners and below the eye rims to remove mucus and tear stains. Do not touch the eyeball. Use a moistened cotton bud or a special eye product (available at a pet shop) to wipe under the eye. A warm tea bag wiped over the eyeball, gently, has good effect.

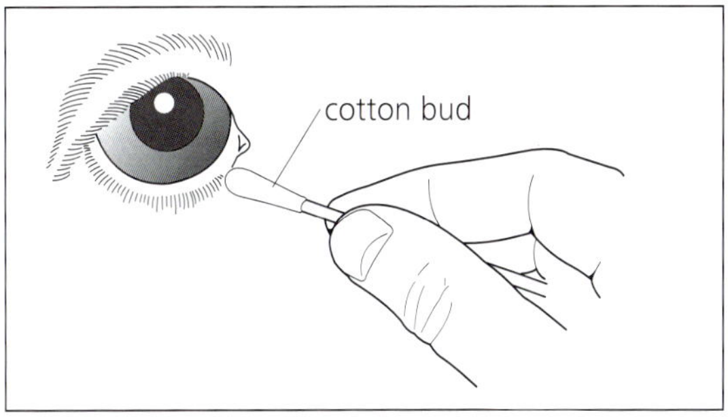

Wiping and cleaning under the eye

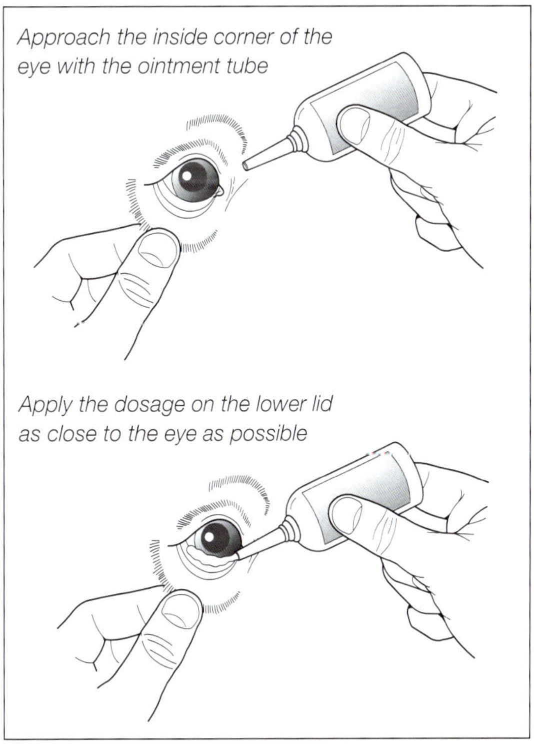

Administering eye drops/ointment

Teeth – Inspect regularly for decay or diseased gums. Bad breath is a sign of a problem. Dogs with bad teeth do not experience much pain but there will be an infection. Clean your dog's teeth weekly once the adult teeth are in, using a soft toothbrush and dog toothpaste (this has a flavour dogs like). If there is a build up of tartar on the teeth, your vet can scale and clean them. However, this has to be done while the dog is under an anaesthetic. It is preferable to brush regularly to avoid tartar build up.

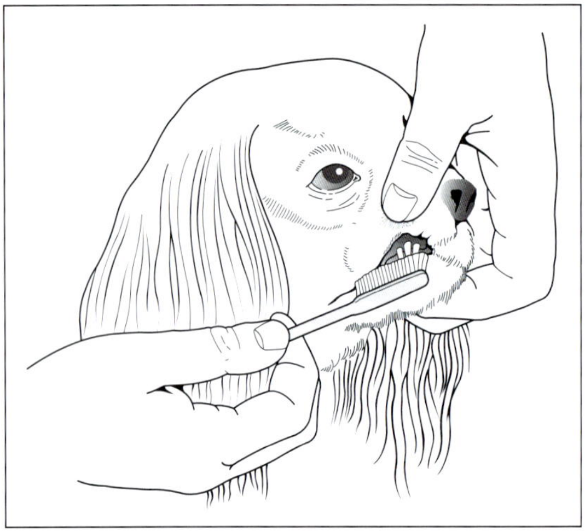

Teeth cleaning

Nails – If your dog does not walk on hard surfaces, you will need to clip the nails from time to time. Hold the paw in your hand taking each nail in turn, squeeze the nail at the base between the thumb and index fingers. With your other hand carefully clip or trim the end of the nail, taking care to avoid the vein that enters the nail near the paw pad. If accidental bleeding occurs, press an ice cube directly on the area and the bleeding should stop. If the dew claws (an under-developed nail, like a thumb, on the inner surface of the pastern region of the front legs) were not removed by the breeder, they should also be clipped.

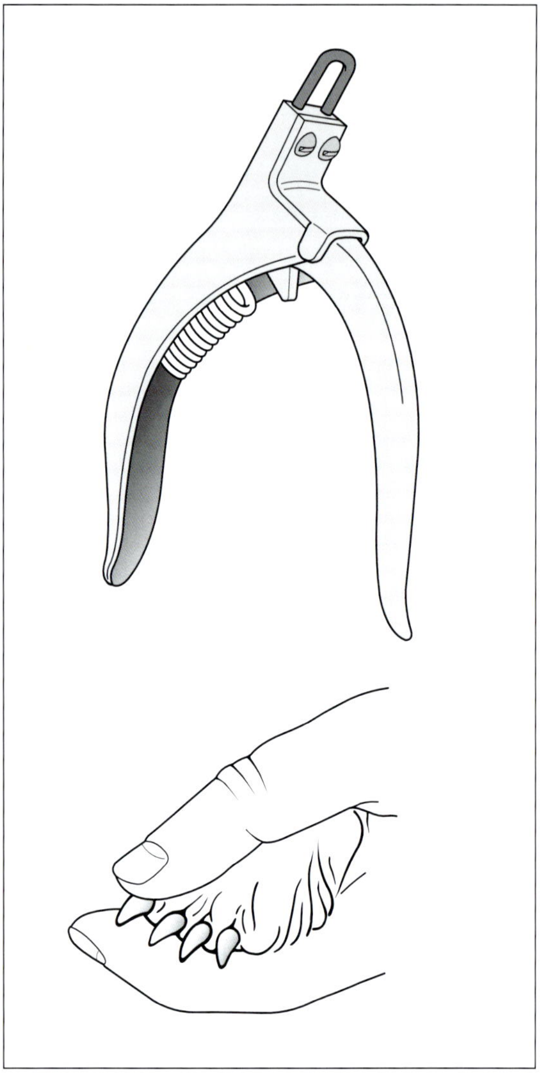

Nail clipping

Umbilical hernia – This is fairly common in the breed and is not regarded as serious unless the hernia is very large. It looks like a small 'bubble' of fatty abdominal tissue where the navel is. When a puppy is young you can usually press it back into the abdominal aperture. When the hole closes it may leave a small bubble sticking out. This usually does not cause any problem to the Cavalier. However, if the bubble is larger, about the size of a walnut, you should consult your vet.

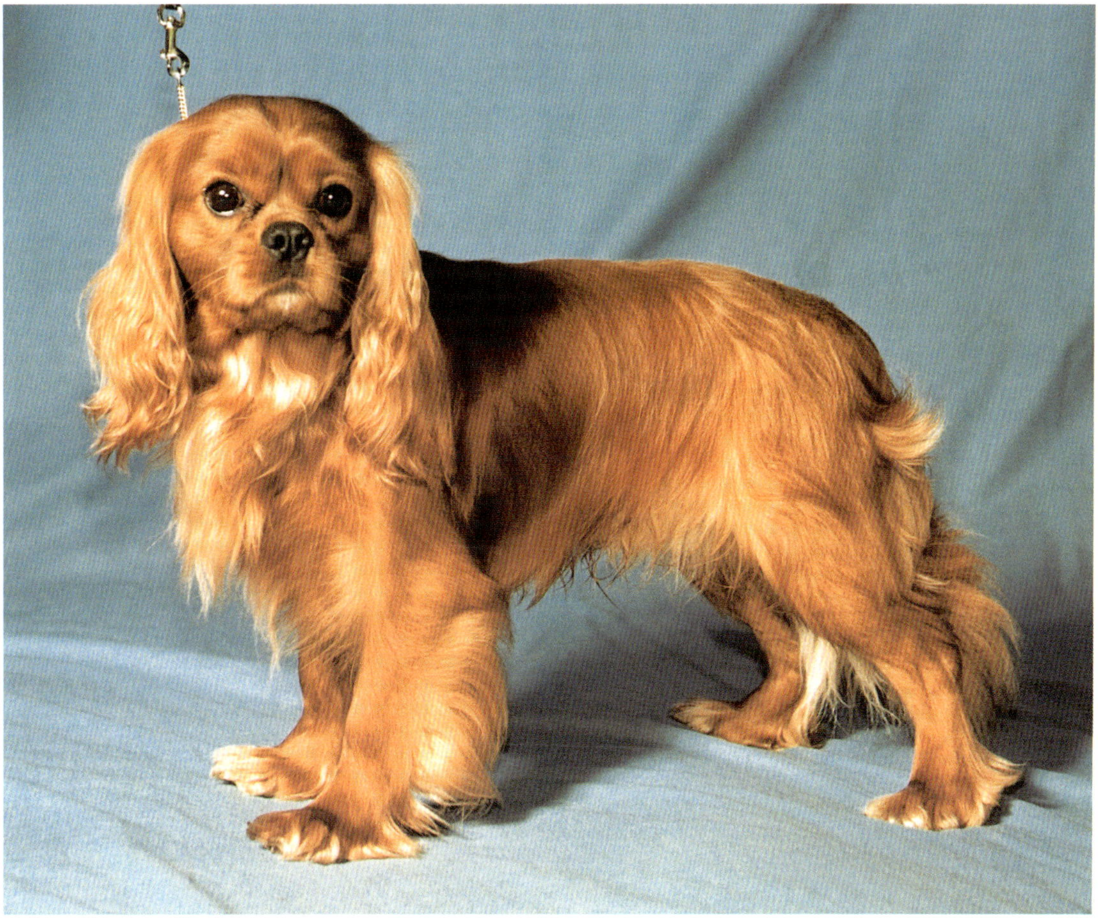

Ruby dog aged eighteen months

Anal sacs – The anal sacs (glands) are tear-drop shaped and are located on each side of the rectum. Cavaliers seem to require these to be emptied fairly often but the frequency varies with the individual dog. If your dog scoots on his bottom and bites at his side, you should ask your vet to empty the anal glands, or, your vet can show you how to do this yourself. If you should decide to do it, practise in a bath at first because a very smelly substance shoots out!

Fleas – There are excellent flea sprays to be bought in pet shops. Your vet will probably stock a good one which may not be available in pet shops. Keep a spray handy and use immediately a flea is spotted.

Walking mange ***(Cheyletiela)*** – This looks like a heavy dandruff on the back along the spine. Under a magnifying glass it is seen as tiny moving pieces of dandruff with legs. This usually affects young pups between four and twelve weeks and, although it is annoying at the time, it is easily remedied. The puppy should be bathed in a product that kills mites (Seleen is excellent) or use a product recommended by your vet. Interestingly some humans are allergic to the mites, and get itchy blisters on the inner arm and stomach, where the pups have been carried.

Black and tan puppy

Blenheim at home

Eleven-month-old Blenheim

HEALTH

Cavaliers are generally a healthy and active breed. In common with all other breeds, they occasionally suffer from a variety of normal diseases and conditions that may need to be examined and diagnosed by a vet. There are two specific conditions that are experienced by Cavaliers but these do not affect their health and do not need assistance from a vet.

A typical Cavalier pose shown by this ten-week-old ruby puppy

SNORTING

When this occurs your Cavalier appears to be choking and gasping for breath. This condition is not serious. You need to hold the dog's mouth shut, cover his nose with the palm of your other hand and lower his head, towards his chest. The snorting will quickly stop.

Ready for a game; eight-week-old Blenheim puppy

CAR SICKNESS

Most Cavaliers travel well and you can take your puppy on short trips to accustom him to the motion of car travel. If he becomes sick, give a quarter tablet of travel sickness suppressant. Most puppies quickly grow out of feeling nausea. Remember you must never leave your dog in the car on a warm or hot day. The temperature in the car rises quickly and it will become hotter than you expect. A small open window is not good enough.

Two good friends relaxing

MITRAL VALVE DISEASE

There is, however, a major genetic health problem which affects Cavaliers and those who contract it seem to do so at an earlier age than is found in other breeds, it results in ill-health and, for some, an early death. It is called Mitral Valve Disease (MVD), which is an early ageing of the valves of the heart. Blood leaks back from the main pumping chambers of the heart (ventricles) to the receiving chambers (atria). The heart can cope with a small amount of leakage for many months and even years, but the condition can be progressive and eventually the heart will fail.

MVD was first uncovered in 1983 by Dr P. G. G. Darke and the Cavalier Clubs unanimously sponsored further research, which led to hearts being tested annually for symptoms of MVD. A certificate is issued stating whether the heart is found to be clear or affected. The code of practice, which is sponsored by all of the Cavalier Clubs, requires breeding only from dogs and bitches with 'clear' hearts and recommends the older the better.

EYE PROBLEMS

Another health problem concerns the eyes. A small number of Cavalier puppies are born with eye 'folds' (hereditary cataracts) and an even smaller number contract Multifocal Retinal Dysplasia, with age. Thankfully, the incidence of these is very small within the breed. The Kennel Club and British Veterinary Association have a joint scheme to examine Cavaliers for these eye problems, and results (affected or non-affected) are published in the quarterly *Kennel Club Breed* records supplement. Because of these diseases, anyone wishing to own a Cavalier is urged to make sure that both the sire and dam of the prospective puppy are unaffected.

USEFUL ADDRESSES

The Cavalier King Charles Spaniel Club
Secretary: Mrs A. Jones, The Old Swan, Carrog, Nr Corwen, Denbyshire LL21 9AY (01490 430554)
Puppy Register: Mrs Monham Brown (01202 420727) and Mrs J. Blunt (01604 810819)

Scottish Cavalier King Charles Spaniel Club
Secretary: Mrs Lindsay Gow, 32 Cammo Gardens, Edinburgh EH4 8EQ (0131 339 2503)
Puppy Register: Mrs Morag Donaldson (01383 880336)

Cavalier King Charles Spaniel Club of Ireland
Secretary: Mrs Evelyn Hurley, 14 Grange Park View, Raheny, Dublin 5 (00353 1848 1621)

West of England Cavalier King Charles Spaniel Club
Secretary: Mr J. Evans, The Shieling, Gloucester Road, Standish, Glos. GL10 3DN (01453 822599)
Puppy Register: Mrs J. Albrow (01453 549187)

Northern Cavalier King Charles Spaniel Club
Secretary: Mr I. Sidgwick, Little Bracken, Corby Hill, Carlisle, Cumbria CA4 8QA (01228 561209)
Puppy Register: Mrs M. Crossley (01422 360372) and Mrs N. Wilkinson (01282 815768)

Midland Cavalier King Charles Spaniel Club
Secretary: Mrs Mary Rees, Little Oaks, 114 Hawkes Mill Lane, Coventry CV5 9FN (024 7640 3583)
Puppy Register: Mrs S. Lymer (01530 831929)

Eastern Counties Cavalier King Charles Spaniel Club
Secretary: Ms Maryann Hogan, Stavonga Dell, 21 Pasture Rd, Letchworth SG6 3LP (01426 670774)
Puppy Register: Mrs Pam Craig (01582 425377)

Southern Cavalier King Charles Spaniel Club
Secretary: Mr G. Ford, The Birches, Goscombs Lane, Gundleton, Alresford SO24 9SP (01962 772317)
Puppy Register: Mrs Paula Stark (01428 751339)

Northern Ireland Cavalier King Charles Spaniel Club
Secretary: Mr G. Porter, Windy Ridge, Ringcreevey Road, Comber, Co Down BT23 5JP (028 9187 2222)
Puppy Register: Mrs H. Lamont (028 2589 8171) and Mrs B. Hilditch (028 9336 2361)

The South & West Wales Cavalier King Charles Spaniel Club
Secretary: Mr A. Close, Lamont, Claude Road West, Barry, S. Glamorgan CF62 7JG
Puppy Register: Miss M. and Miss V. Jones (01443 474070)

Humberside Cavalier King Charles Spaniel Club
Secretary: Mrs R. Mochrie, Hillcrest, Hopton, Stafford ST18 0AH (01785 253717)
Puppy Register: Mr J. Hurst (0191 528 5993) and Mrs C. Baldrey (01406 380596)

The Kennel Club
1 Clarges Street, London W1Y 8AB (0870 606 6750)

The American Kennel Club
4th Floor, 260 Madison Avenue, New York NY 10016/2401

ACKNOWLEDGEMENTS

Our special thanks to all who have helped in the preparation of this book: Elaine Dolamore, for the section on training and Joan Kitley for special subject photographs. Special thanks also to our friends who kindly provided personal photographs to illustrate this lovely breed: Sheelagh Allerton, Jo Blunt, Jeanne Boyd, Di and Lucy Koster, Heather Lamont, Michael Levy and Mark Sedgwick, Ellie Mordecai, Peter and Ruta Towse, Sheelagh Waters (for the King Charles Spaniel).

Cover photograph by Tracy Morgan Animal Photography

Dedicated to our grandchildren

Simon, Thomas and Suzanne

British Library Cataloguing-in-Publication Data.
A catalogue record for this book is available from the British Library

ISBN 0.85131.777.4

Published in Great Britain in 2000 by
J. A. Allen an imprint of Robert Hale Ltd.,
Clerkenwell House, 45–47 Clerkenwell Green,
London EC1R 0HT

Series design by Paul Saunders, layout by Rodney Paull
Line artwork by Rodney Paull, colour artwork on p. 3 by Maggie Raynor
Series editor John Beaton
Colour processing by Tenon & Polert Colour Scanning Ltd., Hong Kong
Printed in Hong Kong by Dah Hua International Printing Press Co. Ltd.